Dinosaur

This is Mr Bean's dinosaur. He played with it when he was small.

W0099595

Dentist

This is the dentist. He knows a lot about teeth.

Before you read ...
What do you think? Does Mr Bean like going to the dentist?

New Words

What do these new words mean? Ask your teacher or use your dictionary.

glue

This is **glue**.

airbed

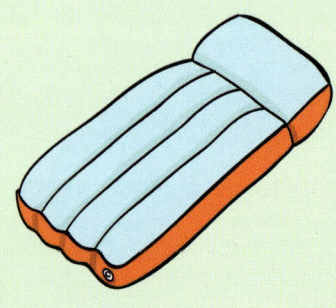

You can sleep on an **airbed**.

horn

This dinosaur has three **horns**.

drawers

Have you got **drawers** in your room?

hurt

The girl's hand **hurts**.

ice

There is some **ice** in this drink.

popcorn

I like **popcorn**.

string

This is **string**.

mirror

The boy is looking in the **mirror.**

tooth / teeth

Look at the dog's **teeth**!

Verbs

Present	Past
fall	fell
sit	sat

What does the title
Toothache mean?
Ask your teacher.

THE WORLD OF BEAN

We wanted to know more about Mr Bean! So we went to his house to ask some questions ...

 Hello, Mr Bean! How are you?

 Hello! I'm fine but I'm hungry. Have you got any popcorn?

 No, sorry! Do you like popcorn?

 Yes, it's my favourite food. Teddy likes it too. We eat it for dinner every day.

Q OK! What do you do after dinner?

 A I watch TV with Teddy.

 Q Do you and Teddy read books?

 A No, Teddy can't read!

 **Q** What time do you have dinner?

 A Five o'clock. Oh look! It's five o'clock now. I'm going to make popcorn pizza. Bye!

– Bye, Mr Bean!

 Q Oh! Can you read, Mr Bean?

A Yes and no. I can read when the light's on, but I can't read when the light's off.

What do these words mean? Find out.
question   pizza

Toothache

Mr Bean and Teddy were at home. Mr Bean loved watching TV …

And he loved popcorn.

Nice popcorn, Teddy!

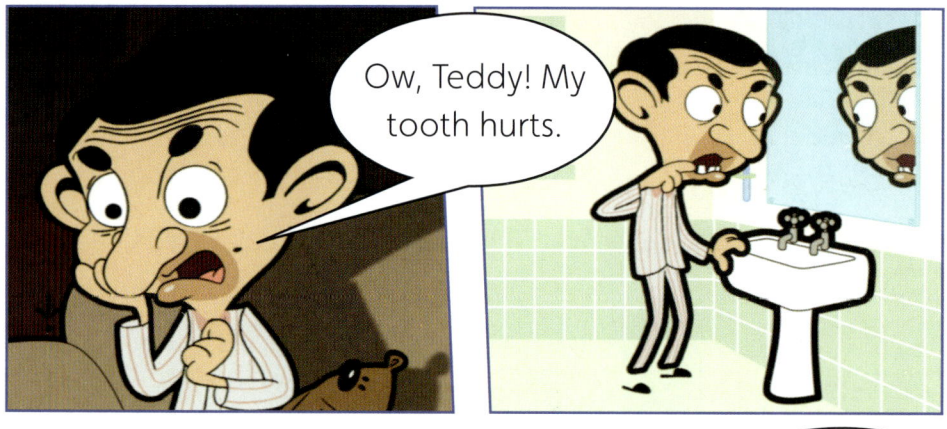

Ow, Teddy! My tooth hurts.

Ow! My tooth is coming out!

Next morning, Mr Bean was in his kitchen.

Ow! My tooth!

Mr Bean looked for some ice.

I want some ice!

Oh no!

Ow! It's cold.

Ice is nice!

That night, Mr Bean was in bed. It was very hot.

Where's the ice? And ... what's that?

Ow! My tooth hurts! I can't sleep!

Next day, Mr Bean had some breakfast.

OWWWWWWWW!

Mr Bean put a string round his tooth.

Oh no! I can't do it!

Let's see!

Three ... two ... one ... *NOW!*

But the tooth did not come out.

What can I do now?

I can take the airbeds into the garden.

Mr Bean didn't see the cat.

Go away, cat!

He was happy with the drawers.

Great!

The cat jumped onto the airbeds.

And it closed its eyes again.

Mr Bean put a string round his tooth and sat on a chair.

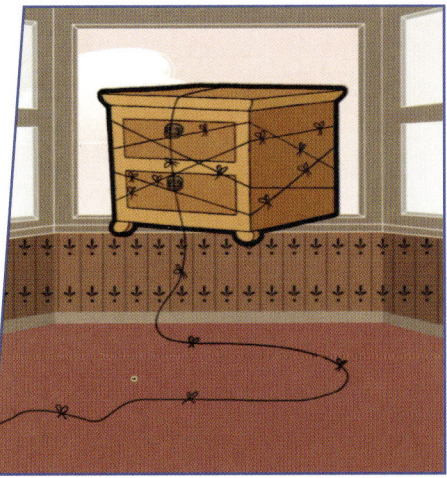

OK! Let's do it!

The drawers fell!

Oh no! I'm going to fall too!

Help!

The drawers came down and the cat went up.

CRASH!

Then suddenly Mr Bean came down.

CRASH!

My tooth! It ... it ...

OWWWWWWWW!

I'm having a horrible day!

Mr Bean went out to the road.

I can see something!

It was a red car.

Oh good!

The car went under the string.

Oh no!

Who's coming now?

La, la, la.

La, la, la.

Ow, my head!

BEEP! BEEP!

CRASH!

Quick! I'm going home!

That night, Mr Bean and Teddy watched TV again.

Oh! What's this?

Look, Teddy! It's my tooth.

Mr Bean put some glue on his tooth.

There! That's great!

Oh no! Look at the tooth! That horrible glue!

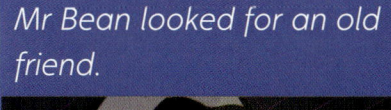
Mr Bean looked for an old friend.

My old dinosaur!

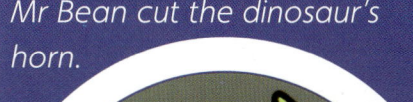
Mr Bean cut the dinosaur's horn.

Next morning, Mr Bean looked in the mirror.

Sorry, Dinosaur. I want a new tooth!

Oh no! This new dinosaur tooth is horrible!

What can I do now?

Mr Bean went to the dentist.

Mr Bean was frightened of the dentist.

Oh no!

Sit down, please, Mr Bean. Let's see your tooth!

First the dentist helped Mr Bean with his tooth.

Here's your tooth, Mr Bean.

Mr Bean waited. Then he looked at the chair.

Hmmm ... Interesting!

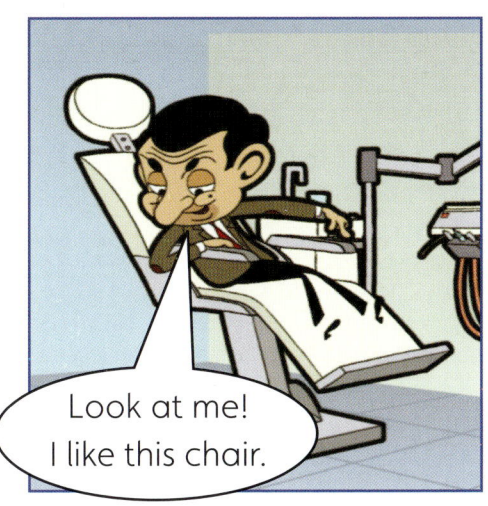

Look at me! I like this chair.

Hello! It's me!

What does this do?

I love it!

At home, Mr Bean put the dinosaur's horn on again.

Look, Teddy!

Oh no! Look at your horn!

I can help you, Dinosaur.

OWWWWWWWW!

THE END

25

TEETH

Read about some
interesting teeth
... and don't
get toothache!

shark

crocodile

Wonderful animals

- Sharks' teeth come out every week – and new teeth grow!
- Tigers have big teeth. They are 7 centimetres long!

How many teeth?

- Young children have 20 teeth.
- Adults have 32 teeth.
- Dogs have 42 teeth and crocodiles have 60!

26

Did you know?

George Washington was the first President of the United States (1789-1797). His teeth were not good. Lots of them came out. His dentists made some new teeth. They made them from animals' teeth!

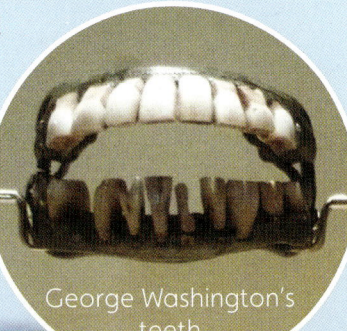

George Washington's teeth

How can we look after our teeth?

- Brush your teeth in the morning and before bedtime.
- Don't eat a lot of sweets.
- See the dentist two times every year.

sweets

What do these words mean? Find out.

grow   tiger   adult
made   look after

How many teeth have you got?

After you read

1 Yes or No? Read and circle.

a) Mr Bean loves popcorn. **Yes** No

b) Mr Bean finds ice in the garden. **Yes No**

c) Mr Bean is very strong. **Yes No**

d) The drawers fell on the airbeds. **Yes No**

e) Mr Bean is frightened of the dentist. **Yes No**

f) Mr Bean plays with the dentist's chair. **Yes No**

g) The dinosaur is purple. **Yes No**

h) The dentist gives a new tooth to Mr Bean. **Yes No**

2 Match the sentence halves.

a) Mr Bean watched TV

b) Mr Bean put ice

c) Mr Bean put the drawers

d) Mr Bean did not see

e) The red car went

f) Mr Bean cut

i) under the string.

ii) the dinosaur's horn.

iii) with Teddy.

iv) on his face.

v) on the airbeds.

vi) the cat.

Where's the popcorn?
Look in your book.
Can you find it?

Puzzle time!

1a Look at the pictures and write A or B.

a) There is a book under the table.
b) The girl is sad.
c) There are two pictures in the room.
d) A man is wearing a blue t-shirt.
e) The old man's mouth is open.

A

1b Can you find one more difference? What is it?

....

2 Look and write the words.

a) e h t t e <u>t e e t h</u>

b) s w e r d a r _ _ _ _ _ _ _

c) n o u r s a d i _ _ _ _ _ _ _ _

d) n i r s g t _ _ _ _ _ _

e) n o r c o p p _ _ _ _ _ _ _

3 Solve the code and answer the questions.

A	B	C	D	E	F	G	H	I	J	K	L	M
1	2	3	4	5	6	7	8	9	10	11	12	13

N	O	P	Q	R	S	T	U	V	W	X	Y	Z
14	15	16	17	18	19	20	21	22	23	24	25	26

a)
4 15   25 15 21   12 9 11 5   16 15 16 3 15 18 14

<u>D o</u> <u>y o u</u> _ _ _ _ _ _ _ _ _ _ _ ? Yes No

b)
1 18 5   25 15 21 18   20 5 5 20 8   19 20 18 15 14 7

_ _ _ _ _ _ _ _ _ _ _ _ _ _ _ _ _ _ ? Yes No

30

Imagine ...

 Your teacher is going to read the Mr Bean story. When the whistle goes, say the missing word.

For example:

Mr Bean and Teddy are watching TV. Mr Bean is eating .

Popcorn!

Suddenly Mr Bean gets toothache. He looks at his teeth in the .

Mirror!

31

Chant

1 🎵 Listen and read.

Go away, toothache!

Look at Mr Bean!
He's very sad.
He's got toothache.
He knows it's bad.

He can't eat.
It hurts a lot.
He can't sleep.
It doesn't stop!

The dentist says,
'It's not OK.
Don't eat popcorn
Night and day!'

Eat an apple
Every day,
Then your toothache
Goes away!

2 🎵 Say the chant.